For James M Orn

Christon J. Powell

Best Wishes for All Good

11/03

Thanks FOR COMING BY

POEMS BY

Chester F. Powell

First Edition, April, 1997

Copyright © 1997
By
Plum Lick Publishing, Incorporated
1101 Plum Lick Road
Paris, Kentucky 40361-9547

Cover design and book production
by Stacey Freibert Design

Cover Illustrations by Jackie Larkins

Other books available by Chester F. Powell

A Kentucky Morning

Chester F. Powell
1437 Pine Meadow Road
Lexington, Kentucky 40504

ISBN: 0-9632886-5-2

Library of Congress Catalog Card Number: 97-66268

INTRODUCTION

All my life, I have had more joy than sorrow, more well days than sick, and more happiness than I could possibly deserve. I have never been hungry because of not having food.   I have never been cold because I did not have clothes. I may have been separated from food and clothes through my own poor management; nevertheless, I had them. For all of this, I am grateful.

The Lord has seen fit to give me threescore years and ten in spite of my often poor stewardship of them. For all blessings, great and small, I am thankful and I do promise to do better with the time I have left.

Finally, mingled with my lifetime of treasures are those people, family and friends, who came my way. Some of them stopped and stayed, some stopped awhile and had to move on but all have left lasting impressions on my heart. And so to all of you I say, "thanks for coming by."

> "I have a little house at the lane's end
> where the rain falls and the trees bend.
> Sometimes a limb will blow in the wind
> and knock at the window, the way of a friend.
>
> I don't jump though and run to the door,
> but stay deep inside to even the score.
>
> Still, there're times at a long day's end,
> when I open the door and just pretend
> that the knocking there was not the wind,
> but the coming by of a longtime friend."

So, if you should come by, please stop for a while, now that you know where I live. I will be happy to see you and we will have plenty of things to talk about.

TABLE OF CONTENTS

Thoughts Penned on Napkins and Church Bulletins

MY GREATEST GIFT

I could give you
a loaf of nut-brown bread
and a chunk of yellow cheese.

I could show you
a little secret nest
in one of my maple trees.

I could open a box
of Cracker Jacks
and give you the golden ring.

But if I gave you a poem
that spoke of my love,
I'd have given you everything.

THE GENTLE GARDENER

Her little garden
Though not immense
Is filled with color
So intense,
That I am drawn
From daily care
To pause a moment
And quietly stare.

I note she uses
No sharpened hoe
Where tiny weeds
Have begun to grow
But gently wraps
Her fingers 'round
To pull them safely
From the ground,

So not one little
Flower is lost.
But do you know
What thrills me most?
I thought I saw
An iris try
To bow its head
When she walked by.

I'VE BEEN LONESOME TODAY

I've been quite lonesome today,
Sitting here on the porch,
Watching down the road, hoping
You might come by for a while-

I know how busy you are,
I understand that, and of course
There will be other days just as
Good as this one.

Oh, there'll be other days all right,
And just as good as this one
And we'll have new things for talk,
You can be sure of that.

Why, I feel better already,
Just thinking about a day when
You have time to come by, and
I'm not nearly as lonesome as I was.

FOR MARY

Oh, to avenge the arrow's point
That pierced the life of she
Who came when but a tender maid
To steal the heart of me.

She who was so frail of frame,
Armed with but a gasp and sigh,
Took in hers the hand of death
And left the mourners quiet by.

Tho more than fifty years have
Passed, my sorrow does not cease,
That arrow lodges in my heart,
And wills I have no peace.

GRASS

I love the soft carpet
That hides the rough floor
One wall to another
From front to back door.

But knowing how quickly
So many things pass,
For something more lasting
I thought of the grass.

Its cover is perfect
For both lawn and field
And over and over it
Renews from its yield.

It makes a soft cushion
For the smallest of feet
And will be my last blanket
When I fall asleep.

THE SURVIVORS

It is sad to think
that this day, so filled
with the stuff of dreams
could not last forever.

All that is left to me
is an unmade bed, and
the lingering hint
of last night's cologne.

The train that thunders
around the distant hills,
hurries you into a world
that I can never know.

Lovers of different worlds,
who meet and live the bliss
of the moment, survive their
loneliness with quiet grief.

SAYING GOODBYE TO THE STEAM TRAIN

With my single eye I saw the steel
Run like ribbons to the sky,
I crossed the roaring streams below
And watched the humbled hill go by.

I hauled the nation where it went
And lent my whistle to its song,
Picked up men at the water's edge
Laboring men, proud and strong.

I took them where the coal is mined
Came back at night to haul it away,
To where the furnace melts the steel,
Over and over, day after day.

The men I found at the water's edge
Who sung in chorus the laborer's song,
Built the cities, plowed the fields
And strung great highways all along.

Those I met and loved are gone,
Their monuments are lost from sight,
Time has silenced my whistle and bell
And dark is the eye that owned the night.

AMOS GREEN

From memories of an old black man I knew when I was a boy.
He sat on the porch of the country store and told stories and
whittled and loved his way into our hearts.

He is no more
At the country store,
At the barber shop
It's the same,

Some of us knew him
Really well
But some didn't know
His name.

They've swept away
The shavings
Where he whittled
Wooden toys

For folks too poor
To buy them for
Their little girls
And boys.

When Amos died
The paper said
That his age was
Ninety-seven.

They could have added,
"He is no more, 'cause
The Lord took him to
Heaven."

TRANSITION

When I was finished with dying, I feared
the narrow passage was not big enough for
the gray box that was to be my final bed.
There were only inches to spare, yet the
workmen seemed confident and appeared to
be well pleased.

The mourners returned quickly to their cars
to avoid the chill that so often accompanies
times such as this.

When the thunder of the last clod had
ceased, I looked around and to my
amazement I was in a large room where my
narrow bed had coasted to a stop. I stepped
out to be joined at once by a host of people.
There was no reference to rank or title,
those had been left on the stones above us
for the sad-faced loved ones to enjoy.

Some had been there for so long that they
spoke only in soft whispers and if they
touched at all, it was with long bony
fingers.

Then, there seemed to be an air of
expectancy, as if we were waiting for some
greater event. It was then that I remembered
having read, "and after that, the judgment."

WAIT FOR ME

If I'm not here when you come,
Wait for me; I won't be gone long...
I'm going into the woods away
to bring you back a present.

Do you remember the mossy bank
where we sat one day looking through
the trees to where the world ended?

Well, when I was there yesterday
I saw a small patch of Lady Slippers,
like children playing under the trees
with streaks of sunlight in their hair.

Oh, there now; I've given away my secret;
but I'm bringing one back just for you.
I'll lift it from the ground in its own
clump of dirt, a way of adding my love.

So, if I'm not here when you come,
wait for me; I won't be gone long...
I'm going into the woods away
to bring you back a present.

DISAPPOINTMENT

Your letter came today
and I saw at once that
you had put winter words
on summer paper.

You could have said,
"I'm not coming now
and what is more,
I probably never will."

The truth could not have
crushed my spirit more than
having you say, "something
came up to change my plans."

I know no more than to give
all I have and wish for more
then too, I held your every word
to be unquestionable truth.

It's really not your fault,
I just forgot that even clowns
who try so hard for happiness
wear masks to hide their tears.

THE WORLD IS MUCH TOO BEAUTIFUL

The world is much too beautiful
To describe in profoundest prose,
I have so little selection of words
Having spent most of mine on a rose.

I can't describe a gentle rain
Or the act of watching one drop
Chasing another down the pane
Then melding when they stop.

To catch a note of a warbler
Requires sitting perfectly still,
Trying to ignore the tinkling bells
Of sheep on a distant hill.

One thing is quite clear to me,
Man too has a role to play
With rain - the rose - the warbler -
His companions for the day.

And to all the beauty nature owns,
The Maker alone knows the time,
Where and when some final act
Shall join their forms with mine.

BROTHER CROW

With more than enough people to carry on
the affairs of the day without me,
I selected my favorite, shaded, porch chair,
and prepared myself for deep thought.

A cool breeze was blowing in from the west
that stifled the heat from the morning sun,
yet left sufficient warmth, a healing balm
for every needy bone and sinew of my body.

I looked up and saw a black crow circling
the fencerow trees in the back field,
I gave in to mischief and with my little tin
whistle, gave a good imitation of his call.

He heard my call and cautiously came closer.
Finally, he arrived at a tall tree near me.
I hoped another call might lure him nearer
but he sat perfectly still and stared...

I was sorry to see him go and he was right to
be angry, if indeed he was. The same thing has
happened to me so many times that I understand
how easy it is to be deceived by false signals.

I wish he knew that I consider us part of a great
brotherhood, that we're one with all other little
creatures that scamper about, trying to get by in
a world that often seems mad with gunpowder.

SUNSET

Standing on the porch today,
I forgot and called your name,
"Come see the sunset!" I said,
And turned toward the door.

"How can I enjoy this glorious sight
Without you beside me to share it?"
You do not come, you cannot come
I know that well, but still...

It is some comfort to think that
you might be watching just as I am
But from a higher peak, where the
Air is clear and the colors brighter.

Notions like this fill my head at times
When I remember things we once shared,
If I should slip and speak to you openly,
I hear whispers behind my back–

That perhaps, "he is a little confused."
At that point their voices trail off...
If I am lost, I do not fear insanity
For that is often our only salvation.

DYING, FAR FROM HOME

For my Brother, Gene, 18 years old, killed in W.W. II

Mom, remember that morning
When I fell and hurt my head,
How I lay for the longest time
Like I was nearly dead?

You placed cold towels
On my head that day,
And in the afternoon
I was back at play.

Oh, those awful summer storms
That came sometimes in the night,
Rain pounded the windows and doors
Until it was near daylight.

I cringed at all the scary sounds
That rode the dark night air,
But none was ever half a match
For your old rocking chair...

Well, Mom, I guess I'm dying now,
In this place I do not know,
I see a little steam-cloud rise
As my blood seeps into the snow.

Soldiers are coming...
One is kneeling close to me,
He holds a cross before my eyes
And asks if I can see.

Mom, you should have heard him pray,
Like you did away back there
When I was little and went to sleep
In your old rocking chair.

NO TIME FOR TEARS

The heart is slow
to say good-bye,
No final kiss
Or softened sigh
No time for tears
That soon pass by.

The heart is silent
And cannot display
Its time of grief.
Without words to say,
It must simply grow
And when bigger grown
It will find a way
To grieve for its own.

A NEW DAY

As dismal as a rainy
Mountain morning
Was my soul's struggle
With the ageless question,
Why was I ever born?

Did some creative being
Have need of a joke
And in a moment's folly
Decide my existence?

As I built my house
And planted grain,
Loved and laughed
And fought for gain,
Then saw youth pass
To end in pain,

I took to account
My pitiful store,
And asked if there
Was nothing more.
I watched the sun
Slide down from sight
And thought, I cannot
Bear the night.

But sleep came quickly
To touch my eyes,
Then morning came
And with great surprise
I had lived to see
A new sunrise.

I set about
To enlarge my store
Knowing there was
Something more!

FEBRUARY

Freezing rain fell in the night
Some average things were cast
In beauty by the Master,
A shame they could not last.

Ice covered walkways and fences
And cellophane wrapped every tree,
Branches bent so near the ground
The wind was wild with glee.

And cracked the limbs together
Then ran through them with tricks
Making noise like made by boys
Sword fighting with their sticks.

Ice that makes such lovely things
Can be cruel as any fate,
When it breaks and burns and crushes
When its beauty turns to hate.

Trees, like human hearts, if broken
Seldom have the will to mend-
And beauty like all passing fancy,
Slips away like the blowing wind.

HAPPY BIRTHDAY DR. KING

To celebrate the day you were born,
we have set aside a day - as we have
for other important and famous people.

Did anyone tell you we have named streets
and even boulevards of our great cities
in honor of your name?

Maybe you know already, but the other day
an unfortunate young man was carried down
your street, on his way to the cemetery.

The story goes that someone standing in the
shadows opened fire on him with a handgun.
They must have had some serious differences.

It's real easy to find the spot, his blood
stained the concrete indelibly. You should
have heard his Mother scream.

I see in the papers that we are "looking into
the problem," but we don't seem to have found
a solution yet.

Martin, are your soft, penetrating eyes, like
those of Lincoln, still brooding over the way
we treat each other?

By the way, what was it you said one time about
treating others the way we wanted to be treated?
That was great, where did you get that quote?

There was something else you said about humbling
ourselves and learning to love one another.
That wasn't in the paper, but it might work.

We wish you a Happy Birthday anyway, Martin,
and we thank you for all you tried to do for us,
especially what you did down in Memphis that day.

THE TALL TREES

The tall, dark, ancient trees
That try in vain to touch the sky,
Give shelter to the nesting birds
Or rest for those just passing by.

They separate the pasture field
From where the crops are grown,
Shade the cows from summer's sun
Or till a storm has blown.

A swirling wind may twist a limb
And hurl it to the ground,
To warm the hearth a winter's night
When the children gather 'round.

A FELLOW NEEDS A FRIEND

The paths get rough we walk along
And a fellow needs a friend,
Someone he can talk to and lean on,
Who'll stick with him to the end.

A friend who has good sense to know
When you need to be left alone,
Then come on back when you need him,
When whatever it was has gone.

A real friend never needs to know
The things you'd as soon he'd not,
And he won't try to judge your value
By what you have or haven't got.

If you should stub your toe and fall
While hurrying along the way,
About the time you decide to quit,
This friend comes by to say-

"You don't look natural sitting here,
I believe you are able to stand,
What happened to you won't last long,"
And with that he offers his hand.

So, if you want to be my friend,
And become someone special to me,
It could turn out that the way I am
Is the way you want me to be.

"AND A LITTLE CHILD SHALL LEAD THEM"

The old man quickly stopped his car
Though he had the right of way,
A small boy was crossing the road
Hurrying on to play.

At once his thoughts ran back in time
When he saw that freckled face, the
Sun-tanned form that ran so fast with
Such easy deer-like grace.

Back to a time when he was a boy and
Each day brought something new, when
People he met were friendly and the things
They said were true.

But as wealth began to multiply, the
Friends he had known for so long,
Seldom stopped to bid him well as
Though he had done them wrong.

He thought of all he had given up
In his quest for money and fame
And came to the sad conclusion that
He must've played the wrong game.

LOST

There was a death recently
In the house across the street.
This morning I saw an old man
Walk to the comfort of the sun.

His eyes were hidden by dark glasses
And he spoke to no one. I'm sure he
Saw no reason for talk and I really
Doubt if he had spoken to God either.

I thought about going over to him
But since I did not know him well,
He might think any effort of mine
Would be an intrusion on this privacy.

The church bell rang in the distance,
Clear and distinct in its toll.
He hurried into the house to dress,
White shirt, black suit and shoes-

"Where are my cuff links," he mumbled,
"And what tie should I wear?"
Someone usually laid things out for
Him--but not today.

When they came for him, he walked
From the house without looking back,
Then I thought he looked rather small
In the back seat of that big car.

THE QUEST FOR WISDOM

In secret I prayed for wisdom
And much to my surprise,
I found that it was lurking
Right before my eyes.

My motive was based in vanity,
"Act wise and be thought great,"
But what I read in holy writ,
Left no room for debate.

"Lord," I said, "where do I start?"
"You just now did," he replied,
"Wisdom can only be attained by
Putting personal ambitions aside.

You thought by just growing older
But aging holds no clue,
Why not start by listening
To things that are simple and true.

Pay more attention to values,
From senseless struggling cease,
Where there is misunderstanding,
Be a covenanter of peace."

The question was not easy asking,
But I think I now know the way-
I must start looking beyond myself,
For a small attainment each day.

A WRONG CHOICE

I chose to make my love go
And break his heart in two,
Then I found at candle time,
My heart was broken too.

That ugly demon who helped me
Make this terrible choice
Gave no hint I would miss him,
And long to hear his voice.

So now I watch from the window
And wish on every star.
I sing a little song to the wind,
"Come home, Come Home,
Wherever you are."

IN TRUST

I saw a little nest today
I had not seen before,
Gone was the leafy shelter
That once had covered it o'er.

Spring is coming soon with leaves
To refurbish the site with care,
So a waiting bird can reclaim it
And start a new family there.

But, birds are so independent,
If I leave bits of string or straw,
They wouldn't touch a piece of it
If they thought for a moment I saw.

They look about to the left and right,
But I understand their actions;
So I leave the material in open space
To lessen the threat of distraction.

I'm honored to own even partial trust
Of a ground squirrel or a dove,
While their business is about survival
They return what they dare to love.

FLIGHT

The evening has come,
For a while we are done
With back breaking labor
In the blistering sun,

Soft shadows of night
Fall soothing and deep,
Soon the twittering birds
Will all be asleep.

And we to our coarse bunks
Will stumble to rest,
To dream we are sleeping
In a soft cozy nest.

And that with the morning
We'll waken and fly
Up above the barbed wire
And away to the sky!

25

YOUR EYES HAVE TOLD ME EVERYTHING

Your eyes have told me everything,
Everything I needed to know.
It was a long time, of course,
Before I understood their messages.

How you scold without speaking,
Love without touching and sometimes
Heal without knowing it.
I'm glad I didn't learn too late.

When they were green, you were thoughtful
And expansive, like the Pacific.
When they were gray, you were pensive
Staring into space or reading the day long.

Some days, I swear they were blue-
That must have had something to do
With an April sky after the rain clouds
Had blown away.

Eyes are the windows of the soul all right,
There's no questioning that-
Whether they are looking out on the world
Or permitting the world to look in.

ON THE MYSTERY OF DEATH

When I think of death,
I think of it for others and try
To avoid any involvement of my own.

I am not affected by the hint of peace,
That being too great a price to pay
For the solving of so troubling a mystery.
Any deal with death must be final.
There can be no turning back once started.
Still, there is a small degree of fascination,
Enough to pique my curiosity, perhaps if I
Could peek into the darkness, then be quickly
Drawn back into surroundings I know so well-

By being curious, I do not mean to challenge death
but how depressing it is to think that I,
this body of muscle, bone and thought
Should decay in the ground, to mingle with
Leaves, cow dung and all that, I try to imagine
Being neighbor to sprouting trees and little worms.

But from what we know, the sturdy oak and the rose
Rise up from such a magic base on a birth morning
Only to begin that relentless march back to earth again.
To satisfy the ambitious plans of nature, man must
However grudgingly, join the mixture of rose and oak,
To intertwine strength and fragrance over and over again.

That is all there is to man except for his soul,
And God goes about gathering these to himself one by
One, day after day, solving forever the mystery of death.

DESTINY

An oak tree sends down its roots
To grasp the rock and clay,
Not knowing that its lifetime
May consist of one more day.

Before the plundering woodsman comes
With his warlike manner and skill
To subdue it with his singing saw
And haul it away to the mill.

The sharp blade of the reaper's scythe
To store for a winter's day,
May cut the flowing meadow field
Into sumptuous mounds of hay-

Or it may rust on a peg in the barn
Because one night a raging storm
With angry winds blew from the west
Almost killing the helpless farm.

When morning came the winds sank low,
The sky turned a peaceful blue
And slowly, darkening shadows formed
As wing to wing the ravens flew.

This truth, too much for me to say
That any ties of mine are found
Of stronger cords than field or tree,
So briefly to this earth I'm bound.

SATURDAY MORNIN

Rain fallin steady
On the new tin roof,
Hound dog whinin
At the door,

Bacon and biscuits
On the kitchen stove,
Folks movin gentle
'Cross the floor.

Nothin much to do
In particular,
Nowhere I really
Need to go,

Think I'll gather
The children 'round
And tell 'em
Some stories I know.

Good way as any
To spend a rainy day,
No one goin out
Or comin in,

Never can tell
It might be awhile
'Fore days like this
Come agin.

RHYTHM OF THE RAIN

How I have learned
To love the rain,
To watch it blow
By the windowpane,

Tho hard to see
At just a glance,
Out on the walk
The raindrops dance.

In the street lights
I think I see
The finishing touch
To a symphony.

Another performance
That gives a thrill
Is the drip, drip, drip
Of a rain-trough trill.

With the rhythm of rain
My thoughts run deep,
And I am lulled
Into peaceful sleep.

SUMMER MEMORIES

Mosquitoes hummin at the screen door,
Old dog scratchin at his fleas,
Birds out-doin one another
Dartin in and out among the trees.

This is the kind of a summer day
That makes memories so worthwhile,
(Tom just fell and hurt his knee,)
"Come sit on Mamma's lap a while.

"Here's a glass of cold lemonade,
It's not too sour or too sweet,
Look at your brother and girlfriend
Holdin hands walkin down the street,

"Tonight they're goin to camp meetin,
(Won't hear a word the preacher says,)
One day Tom, you'll be sittin here
Talkin about these good old days.

"You'll 'xpect folks to sit and listen
To how it was away back when
Mosquitoes hummed at the screen door
An it was camp meetin time again."

REALITY

I awoke one morning
To find youth leaving
Tho nothing was said
The night before.

"See you later,
No time to chat,"
Then it quickly left
and closed the door.

The next stage
At once was set
With actors rushing
To their places,

New costumes,
New lines to learn,
Then, sadly, paint
For the wrinkled faces.

MAY

May is the month of happy hours
Longer days and pretty flowers
March and April oft relate
Back to thoughts of winter date.
But May is bold and knows her way
Across the meadow and every day
She sings a mountain women's song
Of birth and earth and it's a song
That beckons June to come along.

THE COMING OF THE OWL

Last night I heard an owl call
About the time he did last Fall.
I knew that he would come to me,
From the legend of the Cherokee.

Once each year on an autumn night,
When a harvest moon spills its light
O'er the long rows of corn tepees,
He stops in one of the tallest trees.

Great Spirit sent this owl to say
That he has heard my prayer today,
He understood my stammered phrase
And saw my lifted hands in praise.

He knows when I am drawn in pain
But like the rainbow after rain
His promise keeps me in his care
And allows no more than I can bear.

Should 'fore Spring the shadows fall
And the somber horseman comes to call,
He'll reach down to take my hand
And ride with me to that promised land

Where the grass is sweet, the water clear.
You can tell my brothers I had no fear,
Because one night a great owl came
From out somewhere and called my name.

And how do I know he came to me?
From the legend of the Cherokee!

33

THE LONG-WINDED PREACHER ON A HOT SUMMER DAY

The windows were raised in the little church
But not a breath of air was stirring,
Folks were waving their funeral home fans
And the preacher strove hard for a hearing.

I don't remember much of his text,
(Might have been Deuteronomy)
He kept winding up instead of down
Or that's the way it seemed to me.

Then I noticed dear Sister Brown,
Her face was red as a beet,
Her dress was stuck to the back of the pew
And I reckon it was so with her seat.

Sister Brown was carrying a lot of weight,
She raised her fat little hand for to speak,
The preacher ignored her and went right on
About the sermon on the mount and the meek.

Then she spoke right out in a raspy voice,
Suggesting he draw to a close.
"We're hot and tired and hungry," she said,
"And we've heard this before, heaven knows!"

The preacher had just taken off his coat,
His shirt was soaking wet,
He looked straight at Sister Brown and said,
"But I ain't done preachin yet..."

"Oh, yes you are," the sister said,
"You may think that I don't care,
But my shoes and girdle are killing me
And I've got to have some air!"

ALONE

"The nights here are quite long,
since I lie awake through most of them,
listening and looking at the clock. I
sleep all I can during the day just so
I can be awake at visiting time, in case
someone should come by to see me.

"This evening I dozed for a few minutes
and while I was asleep they brought in
my supper tray. When I woke, the food
was so cold I could hardly eat it. The
tea was still warm but some of it was
spilled, it wasn't their fault though.

"One night my bed clothes got wet, but I
didn't say anything because they would just
say it was my fault for not ringing the bell.
Sometimes at night I hear another bell ringing
down the hall and it helps me just knowing
that someone else is awake too.

"I know for sure when Sunday comes, I can hear
them singing up in the visitor's center. If I
was able, I could go up there but since I'm not,
they come by and have a prayer with me.
They offer to leave me a paper that tells about
their church, but I know I will never get to go."

They found her dead one morning, The mattress was
turned and everything including the little bell was
carefully cleaned. They put her things in a bag
so someone could come by to pick them up later.
The paper gave a brief account of her passing,
but said funeral arrangements were incomplete.

35

UNCLE ED

Talbott's lane ran down by the school
Where we learned to read and write.
They taught us many things were wrong
But the Golden Rule was right.

Blackberry bushes and honeysuckle vines
Climbed the fence in great profusion,
And the white and yellow fragrant blooms
In the moonlight cast an allusion

Of a bride dressed in summer white,
Clasping a honeysuckle bouquet
And dancing about as the wind blew
On this, her wedding day.

There were small weathered houses
That sat straight in a row,
With enough room between them
For a garden to grow.

Uncle Ed lived at the lane's end
He was old and he moved awful slow;
But sometimes he'd take the fiddle down
And put on a pretty good show.

Once in awhile at recess time,
He'd come ambling down the lane,
And tell us the funniest stories
Till the school bell rang again.

We wanted to run and hug him
But that would not have seemed right,
Because Uncle Ed was black, you see,
And all of us children were white.

One day our old friend passed away
And to see him, they let us march by.
For a moment some of us touched him,
It was our way of saying good-bye.

TENNESSEE MOUNTAIN RETREAT
(A TIME OF REFLECTION)

Even this shall pass away-
The leaves of yellow, gold and rust,
The rocks that hold the mountains up,
All of this shall turn to dust.

For all my maddening headlong rush
To scale the highest peak or bust,
One day I'll see from yonder cloud
That all of this has turned to dust.

I slowed my step a bit today
To watch a group of children play,
And ran myself, to catch a leaf
In vain attempt to stifle grief.

Grief for things so long held dear,
For time I may have wasted here,
But I've kept busy, chasing dreams
And that's success enough it seems.

For one who fails to dream, dies young
And tho he hears his praises sung,
His enterprise lies cold with rust
When all he was has turned to dust.

37

SWAN SONG OF THE REDMAN

When this was our land,
The streams ran clear and cool
And all creatures came to drink.

The buffalo, elk and pheasant
Roamed the front yards of the mountains
And fed on lush grass and rich grains.

We learned the ways of the eagle
And caught his falling feathers
To fill our bonnets with pride.

We loved this land and its creatures.
We only killed to feed our people and
Clothe them against the winter wind.

But today, a proud elk looked up from
Grazing into a puff of blue powder-smoke,
The sharp crack of rifle fire sounded
Like thunder in his dying brain.

Ah, tell us again Brave Hunter,
Tell us again the story of the trophy
That hangs so proudly above your mantle.

Alas, our camp fires have grown cold,
Our prayers to the great Spirit
Are lost in the smog of your progress.
We, Brave Hunter, we are the trophies
That hang unseen about your mantle.

STARTING OVER

Minister: "Let not you heart be troubled!"

Penitent: "Troubled, did I hear you say;
just how do I accomplish that,
seeing that my world, the world
I have worked so hard to perfect
has all but fallen apart?"

Minister: "Ah, there now, you've said it well;
the world, the world you have made.
Why not start over and this time
bring in the Carpenter with the nail-
scarred hands. He is a master builder
and He can accomplish wonders with
the skimpiest of materials."

Penitent: "I am willing to do as you say, but I
have so little to offer Him in exchange
for his favor!"

Minister: "For repentance he offers forgiveness,
for simple faith he offers fellowship,
with fellowship comes the help you need
to rebuild your world."

Penitent: "Oh, God, I have washed my hands of my
ambition and reach them toward heaven
In acceptance of your grace and wisdom
with thanksgiving that I may start over.
Amen."

THE WAY THE GAME IS PLAYED

Be assured that no great wealth
Will follow when I go-
I may escape the mourner's page
That way so few will know.

"For a chunk of bread, a glass of
Wine, a fire on a winter's night,
He paid his share for passing here,"
If some notice would seem right.

I was early taught that in giving
Was the proven way to receive,
I was not taught that crafty men
Lay in wait to deceive.

I thought if I could be pious
And attend the preacher's drone,
Be careful in my choice of friends,
I would never be left alone.

But when my fortune dwindled
And my coat had grown threadbare,
I searched about to find a friend
But could not, anywhere.

I really don't mean to blame anyone,
That's the way the game is played,
If a fellow was dealt a bad hand,
It was his own fault if he stayed.

Society is such a beautiful word
And dressed in magnanimous thought,
But eventually we all come to know
That the way in must be bought.

Oh, today, I met a "good ole boy"
Down by the railroad track,
I gave him half my bottle and lunch
And tomorrow he'll pay me back.

A TIME TO GROW

Tonight, we sat at the table
And laughed and told stories
Until the food dried on the dishes
And no one wanted the time to end.

She laughed with us
But her eyes remained sad.
More than once we saw her staring
In a vacant way at the door

As if she was expecting someone,
Someone she knew would not come.
She had suffered a great loss lately
And needed so much to be comforted.

We gave her all we had to give.
First, trying to smother her need
With laughter, that failing, we held
Her close a moment to share her pain.

Finally, we said good-bye and gave her up
To the shadowy avenues that took her home,
Where the heart could be alone and perhaps
Now find strength to heal itself and grow.

UNBOUND IF I CHOOSE TO BE

No matter the color of my skin,
I can be what I want to be.
No matter that my eyes are slant
I can see what others see.

Though shackled by a heavy chain
To a stone-gray prison wall,
With thought I can slip the bonds
And rise above it all-

Up to where the eagle soars,
Where the wind blows wild and free
Where a thousand kindred spirits
Are on hand to welcome me.

I can fly to yonder hillside
Stoop to pick a small, wild flower
Hide it among my treasures
In the deepest leafy bower.

Sad indeed is that poor thing
Whose mind is imprisoned by
Chains of worthlessness, of fear,
Whose reservoir of tears is dry.

It was not the God who made him
Who planned a whimpering slave,
He knew the confinement of a cross
And rose triumphant from a grave.

QUIT TRYING SO HARD

How boring to deal in absolutes
The live-long day,
Always deferring to others
Until they've had their say.

Standing tall, shoulders back,
Head held high and straight.
Displaying perfect manners
Never being late.

Try if you can to imagine
An afternoon in May,
Doing mathematical equations
While others are out at play.

I'd rather be sitting by the creek
In the cool shade of a tree,
Watching a squirrel carve a nut
(Unafraid of me.)

Or close my eyes and listen
To a mockingbird in his steeple,
Have a personal talk with God
And not be bound by people.

Sometimes I think I'll quit trying
To always do what's expected,
So what if I "arrive," as they say
And leave important things neglected.

THE SINGER

My chiefest business is singing
Wherever people will listen,
Though seldom in some fancy place
Where pretty house lights glisten.

Today I'll be singing of winter
'Cause the snow is drifted and deep
And all of my little animal friends
Are snuggled and fast asleep.

Before long now spring will come
With billowing blue-white skies.
Then my songs will soar to where
The sleek, black raven flies.

Summer owns such glorious days
A superior time for singing,
With children playing undisturbed
By a distant school bell ringing.

All of God's creatures are singers
Each has his own beat and style.
Nature will teach us the verses
If we'll only sit still for a while.

THE FEAR OF REJECTION

When I saw you, even at a distance
I could have sworn our eyes met.
I wanted to shout my name to you
And ask for yours in return-

Then I thought...
If I could speak to you privately,
And let you know how it was with me,
But you might reject my advances.

The fear of rejection is greatest
When we perceive all might be lost
In an instant of misunderstanding
So I decided the risk was too great.

It would be better to keep to myself.
Summer came and passed, then autumn
And winter with its chill and bluster
Now spring again, a year since we met.

A whole year of walking in summer fields,
Gathering wood in autumn for winter's fire.
Now spring, the anniversary of our meeting;
Must I celebrate the occasion in solitude?

WHEN I DREAM

(This poem was written to honor Loretta Lynn as Kentuckian of the year at the A.B. Chandler banquet July 1996.)

I lay me down in the tall grass
Between the well-box and barn
And listen to the mockingbird
Spin me a country yarn.

I draw a drink from the cool well
To soothe my thirsty throat then,
In harmony with the swaying trees,
I match him note for note.

I've always loved the mountains,
They taught me how to sing
And on many a Sunday morning
When I heard the church bells ring

I'd sing of that Old Rugged Cross
And of His Amazing Grace,
Then thank God in my childish way
For this amazing place.

But soon with my mail-order guitar
and with what few clothes I had,
The time came to say good-bye
To my home and Mom and Dad.

I've traveled all around the world
Since the days of that humble start,
And the people I've met along the way
Are the songs that live in my heart.

But when I'm weary of earthly cares,
When my tears seem never to dry,
I dream of home and the tall pines
Trying to reach the sky

To touch the hem of His garment
And tell Him about my pain,
Then he allows His little girl
To go back home again.

LOVE RETURNS

You left me standing
On the shore
And started for the sea,

The tide bound pearls
Around your feet
And drew you back to me.

I watched a seagull
Spread his wings
And race toward the sky.

But he came back
To his love again
Just like you and I.

THE CHOIR CONTINUED SINGING

The mulberries were ripening,
The birds were all a-chatter,
An old crow came flying in
To see what was the matter.

A tiny sparrow saw him
From where he had his perch,
Like an arrow shot, the sparrow
Drove the devil from the church.

The choir continued singing
As they gulped the berries down,
A blue jay preached a sermon
Resplendent in his gown.

These things happen every day
According to God's own time,
Then he selects a friend of his
To tell the tale in rhyme.

LOVE IS

Love is like
A revolving door
A raspy saw
A shining floor
A leafless tree
A cozy fire
A running stream
A test of ire.

It's sometimes hot
It's sometimes cold
It drives the young
It sustains the old
Its essence is deep
As a perfumed rose
And unexplainable
From beginning to close.

ON THE WAY TO GARRETT'S ORCHARD

I was today where a stream,
Some trees, wildflowers and
A shaggy barn blent in a
Profusion of color and charm.

The sky did its best to remain
Neutral, but the white clouds
Against a blue-sky background
Did influence the scene.

It is really something that
You need to see for yourself,
And if you are willing, it would
Give me pleasure to take you there.

MY LITTLE HOUSE

I have a little house
At the lane's end,
Where the rain falls
And the trees bend.

Sometimes a limb
Will blow in the wind
And knock at the window,
The way of a friend.

I don't jump though
And run to the door,
But stay deep inside
To even the score.

Still, there're times
At a long day's end,
When I open the door
And just pretend

That the knocking there
Was not the wind,
But the coming by
Of a longtime friend.

NATURE'S PLAN

I watched as nature undressed the
Trees unashamedly in my presence,
And left them quite naked to stand
The bitter winds of winter.

Some would die, yet live again in
The warmth of a cottage fireside
Where children unwrapped presents
On a Christmas morning.

Others, with modest travail, would
Assist the birthing of spring,
By hiding the nests of new birds
From the probing eye of the prowler.

Then there was the farm boy,
Who, one day, would lay aside
his plow and hoe,
Stretch himself out in the cool shade
And feel the presence of his Maker.

DEEP SHADOWS

When I was little,
The buildings in our town
Seemed so tall I almost
Drowned in their shadows.

Then, when I grew up,
They were not so tall after all,
I could see clear to the top
If I wanted to.

Now that I've grown older
And a little stooped,
The buildings are tall again
And their shadows are awesome,

Especially in September.

51

MARCH

It's a proper thing to pay respect
To every month of the year,
But March is more like reaching out
For the hand of a loved one dear.

So, if months should have a gender,
No question that March would be she.
So delicate, riding a chariot cloud,
Her soft hair blowing free-

She is not concerned with convention,
Some think perhaps she is haughty.
Frolicking about at night with the wind,
The perception is, she's naughty.

But I've known her so long I defend her
And when you come to know her better,
You'll see she has just come from winter
And going back would really upset her.

This maiden is bringing us springtime.
Listen! She is rattling the door.
Now quickly she's back at the window!
Could it be she's looking us o'er?

Oh how sad - she seems to have left us,
Just look how the snow swirls around!
Now comes the sun, the snow is all done,
And crocuses peep through the ground.

THE INDUSTRY OF AUTUMN

Quilts out airing for winter,
Walnuts are drying in the sun,
I ordered a coat from a catalog
So I'm waiting for the mail to run.

Squirrels are stealing my walnuts
Tho I gave them a dozen to hide,
They wouldn't take one on my terms,
They think too much of their pride.

"Ole Miss" told me to dig the bulbs
And sweep the leaves off the walk,
But I see my neighbor coming this way
Looks like he'll be wanting to talk.

Standing here, I see a few apples
That I missed high up in the tree,
They didn't fall when the others did
I suppose they'd rather be free.

Free to swing back 'in forth in the wind,
Twist loose and fall to the ground,
To be pierced in the heart by stubble
In the night, when no one's around.

The leaves come quickly to cover them
While the seed slips into the earth,
To quietly rest 'neath the winter snow
Then be chosen for spring's new birth.

My, how busy these days have been,
And it's like this every fall.
So much to do and to think about,
I can't remember it all.

53

THANKS FOR COMING BY

For all the rain-soaked
Windy nights,
Snow flakes caught
In the city lights,
The lonesome sound
Of a far-off train,
For all we shared
Through joy and pain,

For all the promises
Kept and broken,
For words said
Or left unspoken,
For scent of perfume
When you went,
Forgiveness for the
Flowers not sent.

For singing
When to cry would do,
For wearing my favorite
Color - blue.
For going with me
To the dance,
For all the times
You took a chance.

Thanks for coming by.

Thoughts Penned
on Napkins and
Church Bulletins

THE JANUARY GHOST

It's a cold night in Carter County,
The fox is asleep in his den,
The groundhog is in his burrow
With only one way out and in.

Old dog dozing by the fire
Pricks up an ear to the wind
That rattles the door a little,
Gentle, the way of a friend.

"Come in!" the old man hollers,
With authority of the host,
Nobody comes, the wind moves on
Just a january ghost.

THE GENTLEMAN

The gentleman tipped his hat
To three ladies on the walk
Who had stopped at that moment
For some news-worthy talk.

Once out of earshot
One of them said,
I believe that fellow
Is very well-bred.

You surely can't tell
From a passing look
Retorted another,
He might be a crook.

The third said softly
Your words are alarming
He seems like a gentleman
And I find him charming!

Seldom does anyone
Pass three in review
Get one solid "no" vote
But find favor with two.

THE DIXIE RESTAURANT

Old men gather 'round
The restaurant table,
The number varies
With those who are able-

They all drink coffee
And some still smoke,
They laugh too loud
At a much-told joke-

If one has to leave
Then another comes in,
That's the way it has
Always been.

If a stranger stares
It's no distraction,
They're fixin the gov'ment
To their own satisfaction.

BLESSED ASSURANCE

The shades were drawn
The prayers had been said,
The children were snug
In their warm cradle-bed.

Outside, the snow
Lay drifted and deep,
Then the moon came out
And I couldn't sleep.

I thought I would try
To describe it to God,
But He only yawned
And gave me a nod.

OCTOBER TWENTIETH

Autumn, the time of finest beauty
All little animals called to duty,
To gather things to hide or bury
Careful to watch out as they hurry.

Watching leaves fall everywhere
On the ground and in your hair,
Hired boys who rake awhile
Then fall headlong atop the pile.

A time for apples, pumpkins too,
A time for skies of purest blue,
Then clouds begin as if in pain,
Announcement of the coming rain.

WHILE SHUCKING CORN

A lecherous house fly
Stopped today,
To avoid my swat
He flew away.

No sooner had the rascal flown
Out into the great
Unknown

Then came two or
Three or four,
I sat still and
Then came more.

After they had
Had their fill,
having gorged
Till they were ill,

Their bellies were
So heavily weighted
(The very reason
Why I waited).

They only had
Themselves to blame,
Then, too, I had a
Better aim.

AN EVENING PRAYER

Father, I know so little of you,
And of heaven I've had not a glance-
Was faith all that you asked I own,
Is faith itself my recompense?

At times like this, in the evening
When I trust myself to Thee,
Not knowing what the night may bring,
Or if tomorrow be,

I simply ask that the darkened sky
Not keep me from your sight,
And in spite of my human failures
Bring me safe to the morning's light.

DREAM OF FLYING

A broken string, a yellow kite
Sailing high into the air,
Zigzagging left and right
Like the climbing of a stair.

My dream now hidden in the clouds
I had not meant to yield,
Since it was I who sought to fly
Away, above the pasture field.

Oh what a thought for girl or boy
To soar up where the sunlight beams,
To feel the rain before the earth
And find a secret place for dreams.

TO AN OLD LADY WITH A SHAWL

The wind blows around this house
And sings in the secret places,
And every windowpane is filled
With frost's artistic traces.

But the sun will soon be warmer
Bringing with it longer days,
And you'll see spring arriving
In so many different ways.

Soon a robin will be on the lawn
To make first claim for a nest,
Carefully checking an old one
To see if it passes the test.

Next, when you least expect it
You'll see a crocus in bloom,
Now, pull the drapes wide open
To let some light in the room.

That little stirring in your heart,
Assures it is spring once more
And you can hang your winter shawl
On the back of the kitchen door.

A GREATER POWER

I wrote a line upon a page
In a moment giv'n to rage,
A bug flew in and drank the ink-
(Smaller than a gnat I think.)

When the little thing was through,
Away to somewhere else it flew.
The words I'd used supporting rage
Had disappeared from off the page.

I sat a moment quietly musing-
A greater power no doubt was using
A bug that I could hardly see,
To bring a message home to me.

NIGHT WIND

Snow kept piling
On walk and roof
Till my address
Had need of proof.

The chimney trough
Was so distorted
Grotesque, I think
It was reported.

Then the night wind
Came on duty
And left it all
A thing of beauty!!!

BETRAYED BY THE CHURCH

Today I followed
With my eye,
To where the steeple
Touched the sky,
I watched as priestly
Robes swished by,
And no one seemed to
Hear my cry.

I heard the sounds
Of the Sabbath day,
Of hymns and chimes
And organs' play,
The well-known phrase
Though proper may
Have turned my
Seeking soul away.

To have held the cross
Before my gaze,
Would have been I think
The greatest praise.

Z z z z z z z z z z z

Good morning Lord!
You must think I'm awful
Going to sleep like I did
Last night while we were
Talking.

THE CHILDREN

Children are happiest
Of the whole human race,
What is greater than a boy
With jam on his face?

Ask him what his clothes cost
He doesn't have a clue,
Ask him how the market closed
And he'll just laugh at you.

There is nothing ever found
Sweeter than little girls
Dressed up in mamma's clothes
Hair rolled up in curls.

She owns some very fine jewelry
From Woolworth's ten-cent store,
About all she asks from life is to
Be loved and little more.

But time moves on so quickly,
The toys are put out of sight,
"Now I lay me down to sleep,"
And they venture into the night.

A rooster crows, it's morning!
The night passed by so soon,
No time now for make believe-
And there is no man in the moon.

YOUR OBLIGATION

Deep in every human heart
There lingers something good
That cries out for notice
Or at least it should.

It might be a simple thought
Having need of expression
Before it expires
Into fatal suppression.

Or it could be a canvas
Left forever bare,
Because a craving artist
Was too afraid to dare.

You would not be derelict
If your talent is lacking
But you could find someone
Who needs just your backing.

A GRAVEYARD IN OCTOBER

I notice gave
To a ancient grave,
The slightest mound
Above the ground.

And wondered who
Should shoulder blame
For letting moss
O'er take the name.

65

FINIS

Deep shadow fall
O'er hill and dale,
My debt to this brief stay
Is paid,
My once inspired
Old writing pen
Is quietly by
The paper laid.

Someone else
Will take my place
And write his verse
From his own eye,
I hope that he
Will chance to see
Some things I saw
When they pass by.

I pray he'll listen
To the wind,
Treasure rainy nights
And often watch
With someone dear,
White ribboned snow
In the city lights.